The Beautiful Advice of Ibn Qayyim and Ibn Al-Jawzi

Muddassir Khan

Published by Muddassir Khan, 2024.

Table of Contents

.... 1

Introduction.. 3

Leadership Through Patience and Certainty.................................... 17

Understanding Human and Animal Motivation............................... 38

Ibn Jawzi's Advice to his son... 51

Chapter on the Necessity of Respecting Sharia Limits and Some Aspects of Ibn al-Jawzi's Life.. 56

Chapter on Dispelling Despair and Embracing Diligence and Action 60

Chapter on Daily Rituals 62

Chapter on the Harmony between Knowledge and Action............... 66

Chapter on the Blessing and Benefit of Combining Knowledge with Action.. 67

Chapter on Patience and Tolerance 69

The Beautiful Advice

of

Ibn Qayyim and Ibn Al-Jawzi

Muddassir Khan

Introduction

I n the Name of Allah, the Most Gracious, the Most Merciful

Allah, the One who answers prayers, we ask Him to bestow His goodness upon brother [Alaa Al-Din] in this world and the Hereafter, to benefit through him, and to make him blessed wherever he may be. For a man's blessing lies in his teaching of goodness wherever he resides, and in advising those he encounters.

Allah's Mention of Prophet Jesus (Peace Be Upon Him)

Allah the Exalted said about Jesus (peace be upon him): "And He made me blessed wherever I am" [Maryam: 31], meaning a teacher of goodness, inviting to Allah, reminding of Him, and urging obedience to Him. This is part of a man's blessing.

The Loss of Blessing in Meetings

Whoever lacks this has missed out on blessing, and the blessing of meeting and gathering with him is lost. In fact, the blessing is diminished for whoever meets and gathers with such a person.

Wasting Time and Corruption of the Heart

He wastes time in trivial matters, corrupts the heart, and every affliction that befalls a servant is due to wasting time and corrupting the heart. This leads to losing his share from Allah, and a decrease in his rank and status with Him.

Warning from Some Scholars

Some of the scholars advised, for this reason saying: Beware of associating with those whose company wastes time and corrupts the heart. For when time is wasted and the heart becomes corrupt, all matters of the servant become disordered. Among those whom Allah has mentioned: "And do not obey one whose heart We have made heedless of Our remembrance and who follows his desire and whose affair is ever [in] neglect." (Quran, Al-Kahf: 28).

Reflection on the State of Creation

Anyone who reflects upon the state of this creation will find that almost all except a few have allowed their hearts to neglect the remembrance of Allah, following their own desires. Their affairs and interests have thus become neglected, meaning they have neglected what benefits them and leads to their well-being, and instead occupied themselves with what does not benefit them, which in fact causes harm to them, both in the immediate and distant future.

Those Whom Allah Has Commanded Us Not to Obey

[And these people] Allah - exalted is He - has commanded His Messenger not to obey them. The obedience to the Messenger is only complete when it is not in obedience to these people. [For indeed], they call to what resembles their desires, and they are heedless of the remembrance of Allah.

Heedlessness of Allah and the Hereafter

When one becomes preoccupied with following desires, [this leads to] the genesis of all evil. Often, one is associated with the other and does not part from it.

Reflection on the Corruption of Conditions

Reflecting on the corruption of conditions in the world in general and specifically, it is found to originate from these two principles.

Negligence and Its Consequences

Negligence turns away between the servant and the understanding of the truth, its knowledge, and awareness of it, leading them to be among [the astray].

Following Desires and Its Deterrence

Following desires prevents them from intending the truth, desiring it, and following it, thus becoming among those who are condemned.

Those Granted Blessings

As for those granted blessings, they are the ones whom Allah has favored with knowledge of the truth, both in understanding and in surrendering to it and preferring it over everything else in action.

The Path of Salvation

These are the ones on the path of salvation, while others are on the path of destruction. Hence, Allah - glorified be He - has commanded us to say multiple times every day and night: "Guide us to the straight path - The path of those upon whom You have bestowed favor, not of those who have evoked [Your] anger or of those who are astray." [Surah Al-Fatihah: 6-7].

The Compulsion to Seek Beneficial Knowledge and Avoid Harm

Therefore, the servant is compelled beyond all compulsion to be aware of what benefits him in his livelihood and in the Hereafter, and to be influential and intentional in seeking what benefits him, while avoiding what harms him.

The Path to Guidance and Avoiding Misguidance

Through the combination of these two aspects [he achieves], he is guided to the straight path. If he misses knowing this, he walks the path of those who are astray, and if he misses intending and following it, he walks the path of those who have incurred [His] anger.

Understanding the Significance of the Supplication

This illustrates the significance of this great supplication and the intensity of the need for it, upon which the happiness of this world and the Hereafter depends.

The Constant Need for Guidance

The servant is in constant need of guidance in every moment and breath, in all that comes to him and leaves him. Indeed, it is among matters that cannot be separated from him.

Seeking Guidance towards the Truth

Among them are matters that have come to him without proper guidance due to ignorance, so he needs to seek guidance towards the truth in them.

Recognition of Guidance and Need for Repentance

Either he is aware of the guidance therein, but deliberately follows it incorrectly, thus necessitating repentance from it.

Matters Lacking Knowledge and Action in Guidance

Or matters in which he lacks both knowledge and action regarding their guidance, thus missing the guidance towards knowing and understanding them, intending and desiring them, and acting upon them.

Need for Complete Guidance

Or matters where he has been guided partially but not fully, requiring complete guidance in them.

Detailed Guidance Requirements

Or matters where he has been guided to their foundation without the details, necessitating detailed guidance.

Different Aspects of Guidance

Or a path he has been guided to, yet he needs further guidance within it; guidance to the path is one thing, while guidance along the path itself is another. Don't you see that a person knows the route of a certain city is such and such, but does not manage to follow it properly? Following it requires specific guidance within the act itself, like walking at a certain time rather than another.

Specific Guidance in Practical Matters

Taking water in a container of such and such amount, and descending to a specific location rather than another, this is guidance within the act itself that someone familiar with the route may overlook, leading to loss and deviation from the intended goal.

Future Guidance Needs

Similarly, there are other matters where one needs to attain future guidance in them, similar to what has been attained in the past.

Correct Belief Guidance

Matters where one is devoid of the belief in truth or falsehood, requiring guidance towards correctness in them.

Delusion and Need for Guidance

Matters where one believes he is on guidance but is actually in delusion without realizing it, necessitating transition from that belief with guidance from God.

Guiding Others and Its Importance

Matters where one has acted correctly, needing to guide others to it, advising and instructing them. Neglecting this leads to missing out on guidance according to one's actions, just as guiding others and teaching them leads to God's guidance and knowledge for oneself, thus becoming a guide and an instructor, as mentioned in the Prophet's (peace and blessings of Allah be upon him) supplication narrated by Tirmidhi and others : "O Allah, adorn us with the adornment of faith, and make us among the guided and guiding ones, not among the misguided or those who lead astray, supporters of Your allies and adversaries to Your enemies. We love with Your love those who love You, and we oppose with your enmity those who oppose You."

Blessing through Giving Advice and Teaching

"I beseech Allah, and hope for His response, that He showers His benevolence upon my brother in this life and the Hereafter, and makes him a source of benefit and blessing wherever he may be. Indeed, a person's blessing lies in spreading goodness and offering advice to all. Allah, the Exalted, has said, recounting the words of Jesus:

'And He made me blessed wherever I may be.' [Surah Maryam (19):31].

This means a disseminator of good, a caller to Allah, who reminds others of Him, and an encourager of obedience. Thus, this is a true blessing for any individual.

One devoid of these qualities lacks blessing, and consequently, meeting such a person and spending time with them becomes bereft of blessing.

Moreover, if one wastes time merely discussing events and occurrences, it corrupts the heart.

The Consequences of Heart Corruption

Every harm that befalls a servant stems from corruption of the heart. Such corruption results in the loss of the heart's right upon Allah, the Exalted, and a decline in its status in His sight. Therefore, the wise scholars caution against associating with those who waste time and corrupt hearts, for such negligence (the wasting of time and the corrupting of the hearts) ruins all aspects of a servant's life. They fall into the category of those about whom Allah, the Exalted, warned:

'And obey not him whose heart We have made heedless of Our Remembrance, one who follows his own lusts and whose affair has been lost and wasted.' [Surah al-Kahf (18):28].

The Punishment for Heedlessness

Upon reflection, one finds that the vast majority are heedless of Allah's remembrance, following their desires to the detriment of their own well-being. They neglect what benefits them and instead engage in harmful pursuits, in this life and the Hereafter.

Allah, perfect and free from imperfection, commanded His Messenger not to obey such people. True obedience to the Messenger requires abstaining from those who call to heedlessness of Allah's remembrance, and thereby to hardships and difficulties. When such neglect (being unmindful of Allah's remembrance) and desire-driven behavior combine, they lead to every form of evil, often intertwined with one another.

Contemplation on the Roots of Worldly Corruption

Whoever reflects on the corruption prevailing in the world, both broadly and specifically, will identify its origins in these fundamental principles (being unmindfulness of Allaah's remembrance and the home of the Hereafter and the following of desires).

Heedlessness and Straying

Heedlessness obstructs a servant from grasping and understanding the truth, thus causing him to stray.

Following Desires and Divine Displeasure

Following one's desires hinders the search for and adherence to truth, leading to divine displeasure and anger.

Favor and Guidance

Those favored by Allah are blessed with recognizing and adhering to truth, choosing it over all else. They are on the path of safety, while others face destruction.

Supplication for Guidance

Allah commands repeated supplication for guidance upon the Straight Way, away from those who incurred His anger or went astray.

Critical Need for Knowledge

The servant's greatest need is knowledge that benefits in this life and the hereafter, guiding choices towards benefit and away from harm, thus leading him to being guided to the straight way.

Consequences of Ignorance and Neglect

Lack of knowledge leads to straying, while neglecting truth leads to divine anger.

Significance of Supplication

Understanding the profound necessity and impact of supplication, upon which the happiness of this life and the hereafter depends.

The Servant's Continuous Need for Guidance

Ongoing Dependence on Guidance

The servant constantly requires guidance (to the straight path) in every moment and circumstance, addressing matters arising from ignorance (where guidance to the straight way is required) or improper action (where guidance to repent is required), and those where the aspect of guidance is unknown.

Ibn al-Qayyim on Guidance

Two Types of Guidance

Ibn al-Qayyim explained that guidance (hidaayah) encompasses two primary aspects:

a) Elucidation and Indication: This involves the clarification and pointing out of the path. It is the initial step towards understanding and recognizing the right way.

b) Success and Inspiration: This follows elucidation and indication, involving the successful pursuit and inspiration to follow the path.

Role of Messengers

There is no access to elucidation and indication without the Messengers. Once elucidation and indication and acquaintance to the path are achieved, it results in:

- The guidance of success in following the path.

- The instilling of faith (eemaan) in the heart.

- The beautification and endearment of faith to the heart.

- Making the heart prefer, be pleased with, and aspire for faith.

Independent and Distinct Guidance

The two types of guidance are independent and distinct, and both are necessary for success and prosperity. They include:

- Knowledge and understanding of the truth, both generally and specifically.

- Inspiration to seek and follow the truth both inwardly and outwardly.

- The creation of the ability (by Allah) to perform the actions required by this guidance in speech, action, and firm resolution.

- The ability to remain steadfast and established upon this guidance until death.

The Servant's Extreme Need for Guidance

Ibn al-Qayyim emphasizes the servant's immense need for this guidance (to the straight path and therefore this supplication in Surah Al-Fatiha is made in all prayers), highlighting its importance above all other needs. This guidance ensures knowledge, inspiration, capability, and steadfastness in following the path of truth until the end.

Situations Requiring Guidance

Incomplete Guidance

Partial Guidance: There are situations where a person has been guided in one aspect but not in others, necessitating perfect and complete guidance. For example, someone might understand the foundational principles but lack knowledge of the specific details, requiring specific guidance to those details.

Ongoing Guidance: Even when someone knows the path, they need further guidance for the journey itself (to be on the path). For instance, knowing the way to a city is different from navigating the journey successfully, which requires specific guidance on timing, resources, and resting places. Without this, one might fail to reach the destination.

Future and Corrective Guidance

Future Guidance: A person might need future guidance similar to what they received in the past to continue on the right path.

Truth and Falsehood: There are matters where one lacks certainty about their truthfulness or falsehood and needs guidance to discern the correct view.

Misguided Beliefs: Sometimes a person believes they are guided but are actually misled. They need guidance to correct these false beliefs.

The Splitting of the Ummah

Prophetic Warning

The Messenger of Allaah (peace and blessings of Allah be upon him) said, "Indeed the Children of Israa'eel split into seventy-one sects, and my Ummah will split into seventy-three. All of them are in the Fire except one." When asked which one, he replied, "That which I and my Companions are upon." This narration is reported by at-Tirmidhee (no. 2792), al-Haakim (1/128-129), al-Laalikaa'ee (no. 147), and others from 'Abdullaah ibn 'Amr ibn al-'Aas.

The Favor of Guidance

Abul-'Aaliyah's Reflection

Abul-'Aaliyah (d. 90H) expressed, "Allaah has bestowed upon me two favors, and I do not know which is more superior: that He guided me to Islaam or that He did not make me a Harooree (one of the sects of innovation)." This statement is recorded by al-Laalikaa'ee (no. 230).

Yoosuf ibn Asbaat's Testimony

Yoosuf ibn Asbaat shared his experience, saying, "My father used to be a Qadaree, and my (maternal) uncles were Raafidees. Then Allaah saved me through Sufyaan." This account is found in al-Laalikaa'ee's Sharh Usoolul-I'tiqaad (no. 32).

Guiding Others

Sharing Guidance: A person who has been guided needs to guide others, directing and advising them. Neglecting this duty can result in a loss of their own level of guidance.

Make Us Leaders for the Pious

The Benefit of Guiding Others

Understanding that guiding, teaching, and advising others brings personal guidance is crucial. As the Messenger of Allaah (peace and blessings of Allah be upon him) said, "O Allaah, beautify us with the adornment of eemaan, make us guides (for others), guided, not astray or leading others astray, peaceful to Your close friends (awliyaa), warring with Your enemies. With Your love do we love those who love You and with Your enmity do we show enmity to those who oppose You." This is reported by at-Tirmidhee, who mentioned it as a ghareeb hadeeth (unique narration), noting that Ibn Abee Laylaa (who was a transmitter of this hadeeth) had poor memory. Shaikh al-Albaanee declared it Da'eeful-Isnaad (weak) in Da'eef Sunanit-Tirmidhee (678/3659).

Prayer for Righteous Leadership

Allaah praised His believing servants who ask Him to make them leaders of the pious. Allaah, the Exalted, says about them:

"And those who say, 'Our Lord! Bestow on us wives and offspring who will be the comfort of our eyes, and make us an Imaam (leader/guide) for the pious (Muttaqoon).'" [Soorah al-Furqaan (25):74].

Interpretations by Scholars

Various scholars have explained this verse:

- Ibn Abbaas: "Following our example upon goodness."

- Aboo Saalih: "Being guided by our example."

- Makhool: "Scholars in (delivering) verdict, the pious guide themselves by our example."

- Mujaahid: "Make us follow the example of the pious, guiding ourselves by them."

Understanding the Depth of Guidance

Some may find Mujaahid's explanation challenging, thinking it necessary to interpret the verse as "Make the pious (muttaqoon) our leaders." However, this reflects Mujaahid's deep understanding.

The true meaning lies in realizing that one can only be a leader for the pious by following the example of the pious themselves. Mujaahid having a profound understanding indicated that by seeking guidance from the pious predecessors, Allaah would make them leaders for future pious generations. This understanding is profound and aligns perfectly with the essence of the Qur'aan.

Following the Example of Ahlus-Sunnah

Continuity of Leadership

Those who follow the example of the Ahlus-Sunnah predecessors will, in turn, become exemplars for future generations and their contemporaries.

Singular Usage of "Imaam"

In the Qur'aanic verse, Allaah uses the singular term 'Imaam' instead of 'A'immah' (plural for leaders). Some say 'Imaam' here acts as a plural noun, like 'sihaab' (clouds) for 'saahib' (cloud). However, this interpretation by al-Akhfash is neither well-known nor widely accepted in linguistic circles.

Verbal Noun Interpretation

Another interpretation suggests 'Imaam' is a verbal noun, indicating leadership. This would imply the meaning, "Make us possessors of leadership," but this explanation is considered weaker.

Singular Form with Plural Meaning

Al-Farraa' explains that using 'Imaam' in the singular, similar to the Qur'aanic phrase "Verily, we are a messenger of the Lord of the Worlds" [Soorah Shu'araa (26):16], implies a plural meaning. This is akin to the poet's expression where 'leader' in singular form represents multiple leaders.

Unity in Leadership

This singular usage underscores that the pious, although many, are united in their way, belief in one deity, and adherence to one Prophet and Book. They collectively form a single, unified leader (Imaam) for those who follow, unlike opposing leaders with divergent paths and beliefs. Thus, following their example means adhering to a singular, unified way of the Allaah-fearing Salaf, making them collectively one leader in essence.

Leadership Through Patience and Certainty

L eadership Obtained Through Patience and Certainty

Allah, free from all imperfections, has informed us that leadership is obtained through patience (sabr) and certainty (yaqeen). He, the Exalted, stated:

And We made from among them, leaders, giving guidance under Our Command, when they were patient and believed with certainty in Our Signs. [Soorah as-Sajdah (32):24]

Thus, it is by patience and certainty that leadership in religion is achieved.

The Various Types of Patience

It is said that patience encompasses:

- Patience in keeping away from worldly distractions by being occupied in worship.

- Patience in the face of trials.

- Patience in avoiding forbidden things.

However, the correct understanding is that leadership is obtained through patience in all these aspects. This includes:

- Patience in fulfilling Allah's obligatory duties.

- Patience in avoiding His prohibitions.

- Patience in accepting Allah's decrees.

The Role of Patience and Certainty in a Servant's Happiness

Allah combined patience and certainty as they are the sources of a servant's happiness. Losing them results in the loss of happiness. The heart is often attacked by desires and lusts (shahawaat), which oppose Allah's command, and by doubts, which oppose His goodness.

Repelling Desires and Doubts

- Patience repels desires and lusts.

- Certainty repels doubts.

Desires (shahwah) and doubts (shubhah) are oppositional to the religion in every aspect. Only those who repel their desires with patience and their doubts with certainty will be saved from Allah's punishment.

Consequences of Following Desires and Doubts

Allah, free from all imperfections, has described the ruin of those who follow desires and doubts:

Like those before you, they were mightier than you in power, and more abundant in wealth and children. They had enjoyed their portion awhile, so enjoy your portion awhile as those before you enjoyed their portion awhile... [Soorah at-Taubah (9):69].

This enjoyment refers to their share of lusts and desires. Allah also said:

...And you indulged in play and pastime (and in telling lies against Allah and His Messenger Muhammad) as they indulged in play and pastime... [Soorah at-Taubah (9):69].

This indulgence represents the arguments and fooling around of the people of doubts. Then He said:

...Such are they whose deeds are in vain in this world and in the Hereafter. Such are they who are the losers. [Soorah at-Taubah (9):69].

The Link Between Actions, Desires, and Doubts

Allah attached the wastage, loss, and ruin of one's actions to the following of desires (enjoying one's share of desires) and the following of doubts (arguing by falsehood).

Leadership Through Calling to Allah

Leadership Linked with Patience and Certainty

Allah, free from all imperfections, has linked leadership in religion with patience (sabr) and certainty (yaqeen). Additionally, the verse contains two further principles:

Calling to Allah and Guiding His Creation

- First Principle: Calling to Allah and guiding His creation.

-Second Principle: Guiding them with what Allah has commanded through His Messenger, rather than relying on personal intellect, opinions, political strategies, tastes, or blind-following of predecessors without proof from Allah.

...giving guidance under Our Command, when they were patient... [Soorah as-Sajdah (32):24]

Four Principles

The First Principle: Patience

Patience involves:

- Restraining the soul from Allah's prohibitions.

- Adhering to Allah's commandments.

- Preventing the soul from complaining or becoming angered by His decrees.

The Second Principle: Certainty

Certainty is characterized by:

- Firm, established, and unshakeable faith without doubt.

- Faith in the five fundamentals mentioned by Allah, the Exalted:

It is not Al-Birr (piety, righteousness, and obedience to Allah) that you turn your faces towards east and (or) west (in prayers); but Al-Birr is (the quality of) the one who believes in Allah, the Last Day, the Angels, the Book, and the Prophets. [Soorah al-Baqarah (2):177]

And whosoever disbelieves in Allah, His Angels, His Books, His Messengers, and the Last Day - then indeed he has strayed far away. [Soorah an-Nisaa (4):136]

The Messenger believes in what has been sent down to him from his Lord, and (so do) the believers. Each one believes in Allah, His Angels, His Books, and His Messengers. They say, 'We make no distinction between one another of His Messengers.' [Soorah al-Baqarah (2):285]

Faith in the Final Day is included in having faith in the Books and Messengers.

Leadership in religion is achieved through the combination of patience, certainty, calling to Allah, and guiding others based on divine commandments. These principles ensure true guidance and adherence to Allah's will, free from personal biases and unfounded traditions.

The Foundations of Faith

Hadith of Umar on the Fundamentals of Faith

The Messenger (peace be upon him) encompassed the essentials of faith in his statement to Umar, "That you believe in Allah, His Angels, His Books, His Messengers, and the Final Day." This hadith is reported by al-Bukhari and Muslim from Umar ibn al-Khattaab. Whoever denies any of these five fundamentals cannot be considered a believer.

Certainty in the Fundamentals

Certainty entails that a person's belief in these core principles is so firm that they become clear and manifest in the heart, akin to how the sun and moon are visible to the eyes. A saying from the Salaf emphasizes, "Verily faith (eemaan) is (but) certainty (yaqeen), all of it."

The Third Principle: Calling to Allah

Calling Creation to Allah

Allah, the Exalted, praises those who call others to Him in righteous deeds, as mentioned in the Quran:

"And who is better in speech than he who invites (men) to Allah (Islamic Monotheism), does righteous deeds, and says, 'I am one of the Muslims.'" [Soorah Fussilat (41):33]

Excellence of Such Individuals

Al-Hasan al-Basree described them as beloved and friends (awliyaa) of Allah, who submit to Him, obey Him, and invite others to Him. These individuals are of the highest rank on the Day of Judgment in the sight of Allah, distinguished from those in loss, as stated:

"By Al-'Asr (the time). Verily man is in loss. Except those who believe, do righteous good deeds, and recommend one another to the truth and recommend one another to patience." [Soorah al-Asr (103):1-3]

The Oath and Exception

Allah swears an oath emphasizing the loss of humanity but makes an exception for those who perfect themselves with faith and righteous actions, and who guide others to the same. This profound understanding led Imam ash-Shafi'ee to remark, "If all of mankind were to reflect upon Soorah al-Asr, it would suffice them."

Ibn al-Qayyim on the Levels of Perfection

Ibn al-Qayyim's Concept of Perfection

According to Ibn al-Qayyim, achieving the pinnacle of perfection involves mastering four distinct levels. The first level entails acquiring knowledge of the truth. The second involves putting that knowledge into practice. The third level focuses on imparting this knowledge to others who lack understanding. Lastly, the fourth level demands patience in both learning, acting upon it, and in teaching it.

Quranic Reference to the Four Levels

Allah, in His wisdom, highlights these four levels in Surah al-Asr, swearing an oath by time to emphasize that humanity is generally doomed, except for those who possess faith and engage in righteous deeds. These individuals not only act upon their knowledge of the truth but also encourage others to follow it. They teach and guide others, demonstrating patience in both imparting knowledge and practicing it themselves.

Attaining Personal and Collective Perfection

True perfection, as Ibn al-Qayyim explains, involves not only personal excellence but also guiding and perfecting others. This involves strengthening one's knowledge through faith and validating actions through righteous deeds. Teaching others and cultivating their patience in adhering to knowledge and action completes this cycle of perfection.

The Way of the Messenger

Criteria for Followership

The true followers of the Messenger (peace be upon him) are those who invite others to Allah with clear insight and evidence. This is articulated in the Quran: "Say (O Muhammad), 'This is my way; I invite unto Allah with keen insight and sure knowledge, I and whosoever follows me.'" [Soorah al-Yoosuf (12):10]

Definition of Calling to Allah

When the Messenger states, "... I invite unto Allah," he clarifies his mission and that of his followers—to call people to Allah. Therefore, anyone who does not engage in this mission cannot claim to follow his path.

Understanding Baseerah

Regarding "keen insight and sure knowledge (baseerah)," Ibn al-A'raabi interprets it as firmness in religion. It also refers to sharp insight, akin to telling an intelligent person, "You have baseerah in this," highlighting their keen understanding.

A poet eloquently expressed:

"In those who first departed among the generations

Are insights (of sure knowledge) for us"

The Comprehensive Guidance of Surah al-Asr

Despite its brevity, Surah al-Asr encapsulates profound guidance. It is among the most comprehensive chapters of the Quran, encompassing all that is good and beneficial. Praise be to Allah, whose Book is complete, a remedy for all ailments, and a guide to all that is virtuous.

Understanding Keen Insight and Sure Knowledge

The Relationship between Sure Knowledge and Keen Insight

According to the correct understanding, keen insight naturally emanates from sure knowledge. When one possesses sure knowledge, they inherently possess sharp and perceptive insight. Conversely, lacking sure knowledge equates to lacking insight, almost as if one lacks sure knowledge altogether. The term "baseerah" derives from "dhuhoor" (visibility) and "bayaan" (elucidation). In the Quran, "basaa'ir" (pl. of baseerah) signify evidence, guidance, and elucidation leading to truth and righteous conduct. This is illustrated in the analogy of a blood trail serving as evidence of a shot game animal.

The Definition of Followership

This verse underscores that those without sure knowledge cannot be true followers of the Messenger (peace be upon him). True followers of the Messenger are defined by their possession of sure knowledge and keen insight. Hence, the Messenger said, "... I and whosoever follows me."

Clarifying the Meaning

The phrase "... I call upon Allaah, I and whosoever follows me..." clarifies that true followers of the Messenger are those who invite others to Allah and His Messenger.

Path of the Messenger and His Followers

If the phrase "... and whosoever follows me..." refers back to the nominative pronoun in "... I invite unto..." it emphasizes that the followers of the Messenger are those who call to Allah and His Messenger.

The Fourth Principle: Guiding under Divine Command

Quranic Reference

The principle is elucidated in the Quranic verse: "... giving guidance under Our Command..." [Soorah as-Sajdah (32):24]. This verse emphasizes that guidance is bestowed by divine decree and command.

The Obligation of Following Divine Revelation

Exclusive Guidance by Divine Command

This underscores the necessity for adhering solely to what Allah has revealed to His Messenger (peace be upon him) as the basis for guidance, distinct from other ideologies, opinions, sects, and methodologies. True guidance, for both themselves and others, is only achieved through adherence to His specific command.

Characteristics of Religious Leaders

PATIENCE, CERTAINTY, and Guidance

True leaders in religion, sought as exemplars of guidance, embody patience, certainty, and the propagation of Allah's guidance through the Sunnah and Revelation, rather than personal opinions or innovations. They are successors to the Messenger (peace be upon him) within his ummah, his chosen companions, and close allies. Anyone opposing or fighting against them is, in essence, opposing Allah, the Perfect and Pure, and engaging in warfare against Him.

Imam Ahmad's Insight

The Role of Knowledgeable Leaders

Imam Ahmad highlighted in his introductory remarks in 'Ar-Radd 'alal-Jahmiyyah,' the profound role of the People of Knowledge across ages. They guide the misguided to the right path, endure persecution and harm, revive the spiritually dead with the Quran, and illuminate the spiritually blind with Allah's light. Their efforts are often met with hostility, yet they steadfastly defend the Quran against distortions by extremists, false claims by liars, and misinterpretations by the ignorant. They confront innovators who incite discord and confusion, who challenge the Quran, oppose its teachings, and mislead the naive with ambiguous arguments. Imam Ahmad sought refuge in Allah from the tribulations caused by such misguided individuals.

Pursuit of Benefits

Understanding the Fundamental Pursuit

It is essential to prioritize knowledge, familiarity, intention, and aspiration towards understanding that every individual, indeed every living being, seeks what brings pleasure, contentment, and a fulfilling life, while avoiding its antithesis. This fundamental need comprises six crucial aspects:

Essential Knowledge for Well-being

1. Identification of Beneficial Factors: Understanding what benefits a person, fosters favorability, and leads to pleasure, happiness, and a prosperous life.

2. Pathway to Achievement: Knowing the specific route that facilitates reaching these benefits.

3. Acting on the Path: Committing to traverse this pathway effectively.

Awareness of Detrimental Factors

4. Recognition of Harmful Elements: Awareness of factors detrimental to one's well-being, causing hardship and distress.

5. Pathway to Avoid: Identifying the course of action that, if followed, leads to negative consequences.

6. Avoidance Strategy: Implementing measures to steer clear of harmful pathways.

Impact of Fulfillment

Importance of Complete Pursuit

The satisfaction, joy, happiness, and overall well-being of an individual can only be fully realized through the meticulous pursuit and perfection of these six aspects. Any deficiency in these areas risks reverting to a state of hardship and misery.

Challenges in Attaining Fulfillment

Common Obstacles

Despite the universal pursuit of these needs, many falter in achieving this cherished and beneficial objective. Often, this failure stems from a lack of knowledge, misunderstanding, or ignorance regarding the correct pathway leading to fulfillment. Addressing these challenges requires remedying ignorance through knowledge acquisition.

Internal Obstacles

Even when equipped with knowledge of these needs and the appropriate path to pursue them, internal desires and cravings may intervene, hindering one's commitment to this beneficial pursuit. These desires act as barriers, obstructing the path to achieving one's desired state of well-being.

Allah's Praise for His Believing Servants

And Allah has praised His believing servants who supplicate to Him to make them leaders who are followed, as He said in describing His servants: And those who say, 'Our Lord, grant us from among our wives and offspring comfort to our eyes and make us an example (Imam) for the righteous.' (Quran, Al-Furqan 25:74)." Ibn Abbas said: "They are followed in goodness." Abu Salih commented: "[They are] followed with our guidance." Mukhul said: "Leaders in righteousness, followed by the righteous." Mujahid said: "Make us steadfast among the pious, following them." This interpretation poses a challenge to those unfamiliar with the depth of understanding and knowledge of the early generations. Some have said: "The verse should be understood in the reverse manner," suggesting: "And make the pious leaders for us." God forbid that anything in the Quran should be reversed. This reflects Mujahid's thorough comprehension. A person is not a leader of the pious until they are steadfast among them. Mujahid emphasized following the example of the preceding pious predecessors, making them leaders of the believers who come after them. This understanding is among the finest and most gentle in the Quran, not to be taken lightly in any respect. Whoever adheres to the people of the Sunnah before them, adheres to them after and with them.

This is the best of the interpretations, but it requires further explanation. It means that all the pious are on the same path. Their deity is one, they follow one book, one prophet, and they are servants of one Lord. Their religion is one, their prophet is one, their book is one, and their deity is one. Hence, they are like one single leader (Imam) for those who come after them, unlike the different leaders with differing paths, schools of thought, and beliefs. Therefore, the true leadership is in what they are upon, which is essentially one thing, the true Imam.

Explanation of Achieving Leadership

God has informed us that this leadership is attained through patience and certainty. He said:

"And We made from among them leaders guiding by Our command when they were patient and [when] they were certain of Our signs." [As-Sajda: 24]

Through patience and certainty, leadership in religion is achieved.

Different Types of Patience

Some have said it means patience from worldly desires.

Others have said it means patience through trials and tribulations.

And some have said it means patience from prohibitions.

The Correct Understanding of Patience

The correct understanding is that it encompasses all these aspects: patience in fulfilling God's obligations, patience from His prohibitions, and patience in enduring His decrees.

Combining Patience and Certainty

God has combined patience and certainty because they are the sources of a person's happiness, and losing them means losing happiness. The heart encounters various temptations contrary to God's commands, and doubts contrary to His revelations. Through patience, one can resist temptations, and through certainty, one can resist doubts. Temptation and doubt are fundamentally opposed to religion, and only those who resist temptations with patience and doubts with certainty will be saved from God's punishment.

Resisting Temptations and Doubts

God informed us about the failure of the deeds of those who succumb to temptations and doubts. He said:

"Like those before you, they were mightier than you in power and more abundant in wealth and children. They enjoyed their portion, and you enjoyed your portion as those before you enjoyed their portion, and you indulged [in vanities] like those who indulged [in vanities]." [At-Tawbah: 69]

This indulgence refers to enjoying their share of temptations. Then He said, **"and you indulged [in vanities] like those who indulged [in vanities]."** This indulgence in falsehood concerning God's religion refers to the indulgence of people of doubts.

The Consequence of Indulging in Temptations and Doubts

Then He said, **"Those are the ones whose deeds have become worthless in this world and the Hereafter, and those are the losers."** [At-Tawbah: 69]. Thus, God has associated the failure of deeds and loss with the following of temptations, which is the enjoyment of portions, and the following of doubts, which is the indulgence in falsehood.

The Link Between Religious Leadership and Patience and Certainty

Just as God has linked leadership in religion to patience and certainty, the verse also encompasses two other fundamental principles:

1. **Calling to God and Guiding His Creation**: This principle involves inviting people to God and providing guidance.

1. **Guidance Through Divine Command**: Guiding people according to what God has commanded through His Messenger (peace and blessings of Allah be upon him), not according to personal intellects, opinions, policies, tastes, or blindly following ancestors without evidence from God. This

is emphasized in the verse, **"guiding by Our command..."** [As-
Sajda: 24].

Four Principles Contained in This Verse

First Principle: Patience

- **Definition**: Patience involves restraining oneself from the prohibitions of God, adhering to His obligations, and refraining from dissatisfaction and complaining about His decrees.

Second Principle: Certainty

- **Definition**: Certainty is unwavering, firm faith without doubt, hesitation, or ambiguity in five fundamentals.

- **The Five Fundamentals:**
  - Belief in God
  - Belief in the Last Day
  - Belief in the Angels
  - Belief in the Scriptures
  - Belief in the Prophets

These fundamentals are mentioned by God in:

- **Quran, Al-Baqarah 2:177**: "Righteousness is not that you turn your faces toward the east or the west, but righteousness is in one who believes in God, the Last Day, the Angels, the Book, and the Prophets."

- **Quran, An-Nisa 4:136**: "And whoever disbelieves in God, His Angels, His Books, His Messengers, and the Last Day has certainly gone far astray."

- **Quran, Al-Baqarah 2:285**: "The Messenger has believed in what was revealed to him from his Lord, and [so have] the believers. All of them have believed in God and His Angels and His Books and His Messengers."

- **Note**: Belief in the Last Day is included in belief in the Books and the Messengers.

Prophet Muhammad's Summarization:

- **Hadith of Umar**: The Prophet Muhammad (peace and blessings of Allah be upon him) summarized these fundamentals when he said, "Faith is to believe in God, His Angels, His Books, His Messengers, and the Last Day."

The Five Fundamentals

1. Belief in God

2. Belief in the Last Day

3. Belief in the Angels

4. Belief in the Scriptures

5. Belief in the Prophets

Significance of Belief:

- Requirement for Faith: Anyone who does not believe in these fundamentals is not considered a believer.

- Nature of Certainty:

- Certainty: Certainty means that belief in these fundamentals is so firm and vivid that it becomes like a vision for the heart, similar to how the sun and the moon are to sight.

- Analogy: The clarity and certainty of these beliefs to the heart are akin to the clarity of the sun and the moon to the eyes.

- Statement of the Pious Predecessors: One of the predecessors said, "Certainty is all of faith," emphasizing the importance and comprehensiveness of certainty in one's belief.

Third: Guiding and Calling People to Allah and His Messenger

Guiding and Calling People:

- Verse on Calling to Allah: Allah says: "And who is better in speech than one who invites to Allah, does righteous deeds, and says, 'Indeed, I am of the Muslims.'" [Fussilat: 33].

- Commentary by Al-Hasan Al-Basri: Al-Hasan Al-Basri said: "This is the beloved of Allah, this is the friend of Allah, he submitted to Allah, acted in obedience to Him, and called the people to Him."

- Significance: This type of person is the best among mankind and has the highest rank with Allah on the Day of Judgment.

Exemption from Loss:

- Verse on Exemption from Loss: Allah says: "By time, indeed, mankind is in loss, except for those who have believed and done righteous deeds and advised each other to truth and advised each other to patience." [Al-Asr: 1-3].

- Explanation: Allah swears that mankind is in loss except those who perfect themselves through faith and righteous deeds and who perfect others by advising them to do the same.

- Statement by Al-Shafi'i: Al-Shafi'i said: "If people were to ponder over Surah Al-Asr, it would suffice them."

Following the Messenger Truly by Calling to Allah with Insight

True Followers of the Messenger:

- **Requirement for True Followers**: One cannot be a true follower of the Messenger unless they call to Allah with insight. Allah says: "Say, 'This is my way; I invite to Allah with insight, I and those who follow me.'" [Yusuf: 108].

- **Explanation of His Way**: The phrase "I invite to Allah" explains the way of the Prophet. Therefore, the way of the Prophet and his followers is calling to Allah. Anyone who does not call to Allah is not on his way.

Meaning of Insight (Basira):

- **Ibn Al-A'rabi's Definition**: Ibn Al-A'rabi said: Insight means firmness in religion.

- **Alternative Definition**: Another interpretation suggests that insight means taking heed, as in asking, "Do you not have insight in such and such?" meaning to take a lesson or heed. The poet said: "In the past generations, we have lessons."

True Understanding of Insight:

- **Link Between Insight and Taking Heed**: Insight leads to taking heed. If a person reflects, they learn from it. Lacking the ability to take heed implies a lack of true insight.

- **Root Meaning**: The root of the word indicates clarity and evidence. Therefore, the Quran is described as insights, meaning:

The Quran provides clarity and guidance, offering insights to those who reflect and take heed.

The Meaning and Importance of Insight (Basira)

Quran as Insights:

- **Definitions and Function**: The Quran contains evidence, guidance, and clarity that lead to truth and direct towards righteousness. The term "basira" also refers to a trail of blood used to track prey, indicating clarity and guidance.

Implications of the Verse:

- **Followers Must Have Insight**: The verse implies that those who lack insight are not true followers of the Messenger. The true followers are those with deep understanding and clear vision.

- **Connection to Following**: The phrase "I and those who follow me" can be interpreted in two ways:

1. **Calling to Allah**: If "those who follow me" is joined with the subject of "I call," it indicates that true followers also invite others to Allah.

1. **Path of the Followers**: If "those who follow me" refers to the path mentioned earlier, it implies that followers must have the same insight.

Understanding the Role of Insight in Following the Messenger

Two Interpretations:

- **Calling Together**: If the followers are included in the act of calling to Allah, it demonstrates that true followers of the Messenger are also actively engaged in dawah (calling to Allah).
- **Shared Path**: If "those who follow me" is linked to the phrase "my way," it suggests that following the Messenger's path inherently involves possessing insight.

By encompassing both interpretations, the verse emphasizes that true followers of the Messenger not only understand their faith deeply but also actively engage in guiding others with that understanding.

The Guiding Principles of Following the Messenger

Principle Four: Following by Allah's Command

- **Quranic Guidance**: The verse, "They guide by Our command." [Surah As-Sajdah: 24] emphasizes that guidance comes exclusively through what Allah has revealed to His Messenger. It underscores the necessity of following only Allah's commands and His guidance through revelation, without resorting to personal opinions, conjectures, innovations, or divergent methodologies.

- **Exclusivity of Guidance**: This principle asserts that true leaders in religion, whom others emulate, are those who integrate patience (sabr) and certainty (yaqeen) with adherence to Allah's commands conveyed through the Sunnah and revelation. They do not rely on personal opinions, innovations, or sectarian doctrines. They are the successors (khulafa) of the Messenger (peace and blessings of Allah be upon him) within his community, his special companions (awliya), and those who uphold his teachings.

- **Divine Commandment and Consequence**: Anyone who opposes or confronts these true guides opposes Allah Himself and risks His displeasure and enmity.

In essence, this principle delineates that the true inheritors of the Messenger (peace and blessings of Allah be upon him) are those who embody patience, certainty, and adherence to Allah's commands as delivered through His Messenger, rejecting all other paths divergent from this divine guidance.

Imam Ahmad's Address in His Book Responding to the Jahmiyya

Imam Ahmad stated in his book responding to the Jahmiyya:

Praise for Allah's Guidance

"Alhamdulillah, who made in every era a period of remnants of the messengers [from] the people of knowledge, they call from [those who] went astray to guidance, and they patiently endure from them harm, they revive with the Book of Allah the dead, and they enlighten with the light of Allah the blind. So how many slain ones of Iblis they have revived, and how many lost ones they have guided. What a beautiful impact they have on people! And how ugly is the impact of people upon them!"

Refuting Distortions and Falsehood

"They reject the distortion of the extremists concerning the Book of Allah, and the imposture of the false claimants, and the interpretations of the ignorant, who have complicated the innovations, and unleashed the trials due to their misunderstandings about the Book, opposing the Book, and unanimously deviating from the Book. They attribute to Allah and assert without knowledge in Allah and in the Book of Allah, they speak with ambiguous speech, and deceive the ignorant of people with what they liken unto them. So we seek refuge with Allah from the trials of the misguiders."

Understanding Human and Animal Motivation

And what deserves attention in terms of knowledge, understanding, intention, and will is the knowledge that every human, indeed every animal, only strives for what achieves for them pleasure, bliss, and a good life, and is repelled by its opposites. This is a valid requirement that encompasses six matters:

First Matter: Knowing What is Beneficial

The first is knowing what is beneficial to the servant, suitable for him, which when obtained brings him pleasure, joy, happiness, and a good life.

Second Matter: Knowing the Path to It

The second is knowing the path that leads to it.

Third Matter: Following the Path

The third is following that path.

Fourth Matter: Knowing What is Harmful

The fourth is knowing what is harmful, painful, and repulsive, which makes his life miserable.

Fifth Matter: Knowing the Path That Leads to It

The fifth is knowing the path that, if taken, leads to that.

Sixth Matter: Avoiding It

The sixth is avoiding that path.

These six matters are essential for the enjoyment, joy, happiness, and well-being of the person in this life. If any of them is lacking, it returns with his bad condition, and his life becomes miserable.

Misconceptions in Achieving Desired Goals

Every rational person strives in these matters, but most people make mistakes in achieving this beloved and beneficial requirement, either in not conceptualizing it and knowing it, or in not knowing the path that leads to it. These two mistakes are caused by ignorance, and one can rid oneself of them through knowledge.

One may acquire knowledge of what is desired and knowledge of its path, but in his heart there are desires and inclinations that hinder him from intending this beneficial goal and following its path. Whenever he desires it, these desires and inclinations obstruct him and stand between him and it, and he cannot forsake them and prioritize this desired goal over them except through one of two matters:

Either an attached love or a disturbing separation.

Preferring Eternal Rewards over Temporary Desires

Allah, His Messenger, the Hereafter, Paradise, and its pleasures are dearer to him than these desires. He knows that he cannot combine both, so he prioritizes the higher beloved over the lesser. Alternatively, he acquires knowledge of the consequences that arise from prioritizing these desires—fears and pains whose suffering is more intense than the fleeting pleasure and longer-lasting. Thus, when these two principles are firmly established in his heart, they produce for him the preference that should be prioritized, and he places it above all else. The particularity of intellect lies in prioritizing the higher beloved over the lesser and enduring the lesser harms to escape the greater.

Distinguishing Rational Minds

This principle defines people's intellects and distinguishes between the rational and others, highlighting their disparities in intellect. Where is the intellect of someone who prefers a temporary, troubled pleasure—mere fleeting illusions or transient pleasures from a visitor in a dream—over a joy that is among the greatest, constant, eternal, and uninterrupted? He sold it for this fading, painful pleasure, achieved through pain and ending in pain. If the rational person compares between its pleasure and pain, its harm and benefit, he would be ashamed of himself and his intellect. How could he strive for it and waste his time pursuing it, let alone prioritize it over what "no eye has seen, no ear has heard, and has never crossed the mind of a human being"?

Divine Transaction and Eternal Rewards

Allah has indeed purchased from the believers their lives, and He has set Paradise as their price. This contract was enacted through His Messenger, His chosen one among His creation. Thus, the merchandise of the Lord of the heavens and the earth, with enjoyment in seeing His noble countenance and hearing His words in His abode, is its price. For those who enter into this contract through His Messenger, how fitting it is for the rational person to not waste, neglect, or sell it cheaply for a fleeting, transient, and perishable worldly abode! Surely, this is among the greatest injustices. This gross injustice will only become apparent to them on the Day of Mutual Deception, when the scales of the righteous are heavy and those of the wrongdoers are light.

If you understand that complete pleasure, joy, and happiness, as well as a good life and bliss, are only found in knowing God, affirming His oneness, feeling close to Him, yearning for His meeting, and focusing one's heart and concerns towards Him. Indeed, a bitter life is one whose heart is distracted, with scattered concerns, where the heart finds no stability, no beloved to seek refuge in, and find solace with, as expressed by the poet :

"And one has not tasted the flavor of life, who does not have... a beloved to whom he finds comfort and solace."

True Living

So, true living, a beneficial life, and the delight of the eyes in tranquility and peace are only attained by attachment to the primary Beloved. Even if the heart were to move among all beloved things, it would find no contentment or solace in any of them, nor would it find satisfaction until it finds tranquility in its God and Lord, and his intimate friend, who has no protector or intercessor besides Him, and no substitute for Him in the blink of an eye, as the poet said :

Transfer your heart wherever you wish of desires, for what is love if not for the primary Beloved ?

How many dwellings on earth does a youth find comfort in... and his longing eternally for the first dwelling.

Focus on One Concern

So strive to make your concern one, and let it be God alone, for this is the ultimate happiness for a servant... and the companion of this state is in a swiftly granted paradise before the Hereafter and in immediate bliss, as some of the spiritually awakened have said :

"Indeed, there are times when my heart passes through such moments, I say: If the people of Paradise are in such a state, they are indeed in a goodly life".

And another said: "There are times when my heart passes through them, dancing in delight".

And another said: "Poor are the people of the world! They departed from it and did not taste anything sweeter in it." It was said to him: "And what is the sweetest thing in it?" He said: "Knowledge of God, love for Him, and the intimacy of His nearness, and the longing for His meeting".

The Sweetness of Paradise

There is no joy in the world that resembles the joy of the people of Paradise except this, and therefore the Prophet (peace and blessings of Allah be upon him) said:

"Two things were made beloved to me from your world: women and perfume. And the coolness of my eyes has been placed in prayer".

The Coolness of the Eye Beyond Love

The coolness of the eye is above mere love, as not every beloved brings tranquility to the eye. Rather, the eye finds tranquility in the highest of beloveds, those loved for their essence alone. This essence is none but Allah, whom there is no deity except Him. Everything else is loved in accordance with His love, thus loved for His sake. He is not loved alongside, for loving alongside Him constitutes partnership, whereas loving for His sake is unity.

The Concept of Love and Unity

The polytheist takes... rivals besides Allah whom he loves as he loves Allah, while the monotheist loves for the sake of Allah, hates for the sake of Allah, and acts for Allah and refrains for Allah. The entirety of religion revolves around these four principles: love, hate, and the consequent actions, deeds, giving, and withholding. Whoever completes all of this for Allah has completed faith, and any deficiency in it implies a shortfall in the servant's faith.

The Meaning of Eyes' Contentment Beyond Mere Likings

What the eye finds contentment in is higher than mere desires, for prayer is the delight of the lovers' eyes in this world, due to its essence of intimate supplication, without which the eyes do not find contentment, nor do hearts settle, nor do souls find tranquility except in Him. Enjoying His remembrance, humbling oneself and surrendering to Him, drawing near to Him, especially in the state of prostration, which is the closest a servant can be to his Lord. Hence, the Prophet (peace be upon him) said, "O Bilal, comfort us with prayer", so understand that his peace is in prayer, as he informed that the coolness of his eyes is in it. Where is this in the saying of the one who claims, "We pray and relax from prayer!"

The Lover Finds Peace and Delight in Prayer

The lover's peace and the delight of his eyes are in prayer, while the heedless one who turns away has no share in that. Indeed, prayer is burdensome for him, when he stands in it as if he is on burning coals until he gets rid of it.

When a servant finds comfort for his eyes in something and his heart finds solace in it, separating from it becomes difficult for him. The affected one, whose heart is empty of Allah and the Hereafter, afflicted with love for the world, finds prayer difficult and dislikes its length, despite his health and his lack of preoccupation!

It Must Be Known

It should be known that the prayer in which the eye finds contentment and the heart finds rest is the one that encompasses six elements:

First Element: Sincerity

It is that the bearer of it and the one who invites to it have the desire of the servant for Allah, and his love for Him, seeking His pleasure, drawing near to Him, and complying with His command, so that the motive for it is not one of the worldly desires, but it is sought for the sake of the highest countenance of his Lord, out of love for Him and fear of His punishment, hoping for His forgiveness and reward.

Second Element: The Element of Truthfulness

It is that he empties his heart for Allah in it, and exerts his effort in turning towards Him in it sincerely, gathering his heart upon it and performing it in the best and most complete manner, outwardly and inwardly. For prayer has both outward actions seen and audible words, and inwardly it involves humility, vigilance, emptying the heart for Allah, and total devotion to Him, such that his heart does not turn to anyone else. This is akin to the soul for the body, for when it lacks the soul, it becomes like a body without a soul in it. Shouldn't the servant feel ashamed to face his Lord with such a state! Therefore, prayer which completes its outward and inward aspects ascends, and it has a light and evidence like the light of the sun until it is presented before Allah [and He is pleased with it] and accepts it, saying (the prayer says to the one who prayed it), "May Allah protect you as you have protected me".

Third Element: The Element of Following and Emulation

It is that he earnestly strives to emulate the Prophet (peace be upon him) in his prayer and prays as he used to pray, disregarding what people have introduced into prayer in terms of additions, deficiencies, and postures that were not reported from the Messenger of Allah nor from any of his companions. He does not adhere to the opinions of those who permit themselves to stand with the least they consider obligatory, while others may have disagreed with them on that and obligated what they neglected. Perhaps the established narrations and the Prophetic tradition are on their side, and they do not pay attention to that, saying, "We follow the school of so-and-so". This does not absolve before Allah nor does it serve as an excuse for those who neglect what they know from the Sunnah with them. Indeed, Allah - glorified be He - has commanded obedience to His Messenger and following him alone, not following anyone else. Others are obeyed only if they command what the Messenger commanded, and everyone besides the Messenger is either taken from his statement or abandoned.

Fourth Element: The Element of Excellence

It is the element of vigilance, which is that he worships Allah as if he sees Him. This element arises only from the perfection of faith in Allah, His names, and His attributes, to the extent that he sees Allah - glorified be He - above His heavens, established upon His Throne, speaking with His command and prohibition, and managing the affairs of His creation. The command descends from Him and ascends to Him, and the deeds and souls of the servants are presented before Him upon their meeting with Him. He witnesses all of this with his heart and witnesses His names and attributes, witnessing His existence as the Sustainer, Living, All-Hearing, All-Seeing, Mighty, Wise, Commanding, Prohibiting, Loving [and Hating, Pleased], and Displeased, [Doing as He Wills, and Judging as He Desires while He is above His Throne], nothing of the deeds of the servants or their innermost thoughts is hidden from Him, but He knows the treachery of the eyes and what the hearts conceal.

And the element of excellence is the foundation of all actions of the hearts, for it necessitates modesty, reverence, glorification, fear, love, repentance, reliance, submission to Allah - glorified be He -, and humility before Him ; it cuts off suspicions and the chatter of the self, and unites the heart and concerns upon Allah.

So the share of the servant from proximity to Allah is according to his share of the station of excellence, and prayers vary accordingly, such that between the prayer of two men there is a difference in excellence as vast as that between the heavens and the earth, in their standing, bowing, and prostration.

Fifth Element: The Element of Gratitude

It is to witness that gratitude is for Allah - glorified be He -, for He established it in this station and its people are for Him. He enabled his heart and body to serve Him. Were it not for Allah - glorified be He -, none of that would have been, just as the Companions used to declare in the presence of the Prophet (peace and blessings of Allah be upon him), saying:

"By Allah, had it not been for Allah, we would not have been guided, nor be able to give charity, nor perform the prayer". Allah - exalted is He - says: They consider it a favor to you that they have embraced Islam. Say, "Do not consider your Islam a favor to me. Rather, Allah has conferred favor upon you that He has guided you to the faith, if you should be truthful." [Al-Hujurat: 17]. Thus, Allah - glorified be He - is the One who made the Muslim a Muslim and the prayerful one who prays, as the Prophet Ibrahim (peace be upon him) said: Our Lord, make us Muslims [in submission] to You and from our descendants a Muslim [community] to You [Al-Baqarah: 128], and he said: My Lord, make me an establisher of prayer, and [many] from my descendants [Ibrahim: 40].

So gratitude is for Allah alone in that He made His servant steadfast in His obedience. This is among His greatest blessings upon him.

And He, exalted is He, says: And whatever you have of favor - it is from Allah [An-Nahl: 53], and He says: But Allah has endeared to you the faith and has made it pleasing in your hearts and has made hateful to you disbelief, defiance and disobedience. Those are the [rightly] guided [Al-Hujurat: 7].

This element is among the greatest and most beneficial elements for the servant, and the greater the servant's monotheism, the more complete his share from this element.

Among its benefits is that it places a barrier between the heart and being amazed by the action and its sight. When he witnesses that Allah - glorified be He - is the One who facilitated it for him, aided him towards it, and guided him to it, this witnessing preoccupies him from seeing it, being fascinated by it, and showing it off to people, thus it is lifted from his heart; he is not amazed by it, nor does he boast about it or show off. This is the nature of elevated actions.

Another benefit is that it adds praise [to Allah] and ascribes it rightfully to Him. He does not attribute praise to himself, but all praise is for Allah, just as he witnesses all blessings are from Him, all favors are His, and all goodness is in His hands. In the perfection of monotheism, his foot does not settle in the station of monotheism except by knowing that and witnessing it. When he knows it and firmly establishes it in himself, it becomes a element for him, and when it becomes a element in his heart, it yields love for Him, intimacy with Allah, longing for His meeting, and delight in His remembrance and obedience, which has no comparison with the highest delights of this world.

And what good does a person have in his life if his heart is not directed towards this and the path to reaching it is blocked from him, but rather it is as Allah said: Leave them to eat and enjoy and be diverted by [false] hope; for they will come to know [Al-Hijr: 3].

Sixth Element: The Element of Shortcomings

And that if the servant exerted himself in fulfilling the command to the utmost effort and expended his capacity, he would still fall short. The right of Allah - glorified be He - upon him is greater, and what is fitting for him is to respond with obedience, servitude, and service far beyond that. His greatness and majesty - glorified be He - necessitate from servitude what befits it.

When kings and their servants are treated with reverence, respect, honor, modesty, awe, fear, and sincerity, so they dedicate their hearts and limbs to them, then the Owner of kings and the Lord of the heavens and the earth is more deserving to be treated with that, [indeed], many times over.

If the servant witnesses from himself that he did not [fulfill] the right of his Lord in his servitude, nor even come close to it, he knows his shortcomings, and it is beyond his capacity except to seek forgiveness and apologize for his shortcomings, negligence, and failure to fulfill what is due to Him. Until He forgives him for his servitude and pardons him in it, he is more in need to seek its reward from Him. If he fulfills it as it should be, then it would be rightfully due upon him by the nature of servitude. Indeed, the servant's action and service to his master are rightfully due upon him because he is His slave and owned by Him. Thus, if He rewards him for it, it is purely out of favor and grace and kindness towards him that the servant does not deserve upon Him.

FROM HERE, THE MEANING of the Prophet's statement (peace and blessings of Allah be upon him) is understood: "None of you will enter Paradise by his deeds." They said, "Not even you, O Messenger of Allah?" He said, "Not even me, unless Allah envelops me with His mercy and grace".

Anas ibn Malik (Allah be pleased with him) said: "On the Day of Resurrection, three registers will be presented to the servant: a register containing his good deeds, a register containing his bad deeds, and a register of the blessings that Allah bestowed upon him. The Lord - exalted is He - will say to His blessing: Take your right from My servant's good deeds. The smallest of them will arise and exhaust his good deeds. Then it will say, 'By Your honor, I have not received my full right yet.' If Allah wills to have mercy on His servant, He will bestow His blessings upon him, forgive his sins, and multiply his good deeds." [This is confirmed] from Anas. This demonstrates the comprehensive knowledge of the Companions about their Lord and His rights upon them, just as they were the most knowledgeable of the nation about their Prophet and his Sunnah and religion. Indeed, in this narration there is knowledge and understanding that only those with deep insight and knowledge of Allah, His names, attributes, and rights can comprehend. From here, the Prophet's statement (peace and blessings of Allah be upon him) in the hadith narrated by Abu Dawood and Imam Ahmad, from the narration of Zaid ibn Thabit, Hudhayfah, and others is understood: "If Allah were to punish the inhabitants of His heavens and the inhabitants of His earth, He would punish them and He is not unjust to them. And if He were to have mercy on them, His mercy would be better for them than their deeds."

There are four essential matters:

- Correct intention
- Prevailing strength

- Desire and
- Fear

So these four are the foundations [of] this matter. And whatever enters upon the servant of deficiency in his faith, conditions, outward appearance, and inward state, it is from the deficiency of these four or a deficiency in some of them.

Let the discerning person contemplate these four things, and let him make them his path and behavior, and let him build upon them his knowledge, actions, words, and conditions. For what results, results only from them, and what fails, fails only from lacking them.

[And Allah knows best]. Allah is the one sought for help, and upon Him we rely, and to Him we aspire. He is the one responsible to grant us success and our brethren among the people of Sunnah to achieve it in knowledge [and action]. Indeed, He is sufficient for that and the best disposer of affairs.

Ibn Jawzi's Advice to his son

raise and Gratitude

Praise be to Allah, who created the first father from dust, brought forth his descendants from loins and wombs, strengthened clans through kinship and lineages, blessed us with knowledge and understanding of correctness, perfected upbringing in childhood, preservation in youth, and granted us offspring through whom we seek the immediate reward.

Supplication from Ibrahim (peace be upon him)

"Our Lord, make me an establisher of prayer, and [many] from my descendants. Our Lord, and accept my supplication. Our Lord, forgive me and my parents and the believers the Day the account is established." [Surah Ibrahim, 14:40-41].

A Father's Reflection and Supplication

After acknowledging the honor of marriage and the blessing of children, I made a fervent supplication to Allah, asking for ten children. Allah blessed me with them—five boys and five girls. Two of the girls and four of the boys passed away, leaving me with only my son, Abi al-Qasim. I beseeched Allah to grant him righteousness and success in life.

Concern for Education and Guidance

Later, I observed in him a slackening in zeal for seeking knowledge. I wrote this letter to encourage him in the pursuit of knowledge, to guide him on the path of acquiring knowledge, and to remind him to rely on the guidance of the Almighty. I am aware that Allah does not forsake those whom He guides nor misguide those whom He supports. As Allah has said, "And enjoin upon each other truth and enjoin upon each other patience." [Surah al-Asr, 103:3]. And He has said, "So remind, if the reminder should benefit." [Surah al-Ala, 87:9]. There is no power or strength except with Allah, the Most High, the Most Great.

Chapter on the Excellence of Intellect, Responsibility of Accountability, and Encouragement for Virtue Seeking

Know, my son, may Allah grant you success, that Allah has distinguished humans with intellect only so that they may act according to it. Therefore, engage your intellect, activate your thoughts, and introspect. Learn with certainty that you are a created being burdened with responsibilities, obligated to fulfill duties. The two recording angels are documenting your words and glances. Every breath of the living person moves them closer to their appointed time. The duration of life in this world is brief, while confinement in the graves is lengthy, and punishment awaits those who follow their whims and desires. Where is the pleasure of yesterday? It has departed, leaving behind regret. Where is the desire of the ego? It has humbled its head and weakened its resolve.

No one who finds happiness does so except by opposing their desires, and no one who becomes miserable does so except by prioritizing worldly gains. Reflect on those who came before, whether kings or ascetics. Where is the pleasure of the former, and where is the hardship of the latter? Only abundant rewards and beautiful remembrance await the righteous. As for the ugly discourse and severe punishment, they are reserved for the disobedient. It is as if those who were satiated never truly satisfied, and those who were hungry never truly starved.

The Harm of Laziness in Virtue and the Love of Comfort

Laziness in pursuing virtues is a terrible companion, and the love of comfort leads to regret greater than any pleasure. Therefore, be vigilant and exert yourself. Know that performing obligatory duties and avoiding prohibitions is essential, for when a person transgresses, the Fire awaits them.

Seeking Virtues is the Ultimate Goal of the Diligent

Understand that seeking virtues is the ultimate aim of those who strive. Virtues vary among people; some see virtue in asceticism from worldly affairs, while others view it in devoted worship. In reality, complete virtues are only achieved through the combination of knowledge and action. When these are attained, they elevate the seeker to realizing knowledge of the Creator, inspiring love, fear, and longing for Him. That is the ultimate goal, and according to one's determination, aspirations are achieved. Not every seeker attains their goal, but every servant must strive. Allah facilitates everything for what it was created for, and He is the one whose help is sought.

Foundations and Pillars of Knowledge

The first thing to consider is knowledge of Allah Almighty through evidence. It is known that anyone who sees the raised heavens, the laid-out earth, and the intricately designed structures, especially their own body, understands that there must be a Creator for the creation and a Builder for the built.

Reflection on the Proof of the Truthfulness of the Prophet

Then he should contemplate the proof of the truthfulness of the Prophet Muhammad (peace be upon him), and the greatest proof is the Quran, which challenges mankind to produce a chapter like it.

Once he affirms the existence of the Creator and the truthfulness of the Prophet Muhammad (peace be upon him), he must submit himself wholeheartedly to the Shariah. Failure to do so indicates a flaw in his belief.

Knowledge of Religious Obligations

He should then learn about what is obligatory upon him such as ablution, prayer, zakat if he possesses wealth, Hajj, and other religious duties. After understanding the obligations and fulfilling them, a person of ambition should strive towards virtues.

Engagement with Quran, Hadith, and Biography

He should immerse himself in memorizing and interpreting the Quran, studying the sayings of the Prophet Muhammad (peace be upon him), and learning about his life and the lives of his companions and subsequent scholars. This pursuit allows him to reach the highest ranks.

Understanding of Language and Grammar

It is essential to understand the basics of linguistics and grammar, particularly for proper speech.

Jurisprudence (Fiqh) is the Mother of Sciences

Jurisprudence is the foundation of knowledge, and its teachings are both sweet and comprehensive in benefit.

I have organized in these writings and others from various compilations that suffice beyond all the writings of the ancients and others, by the grace and favor of Allah. Thus, I have enriched you without the need for seeking numerous books or compiling efforts.

No ambition stands still without diminishment, for when ambition rises, it does not settle for less.

I have come to know through evidence that ambition is inherent in humans, although sometimes ambitions vary. When encouraged, they advance.

If you perceive any weakness within yourself, seek the generous provider; if any laziness, turn to the One who grants success. You will not attain goodness except through His obedience, and no good will elude you except through disobedience. Who has ever committed to Him and not realized every intention? Who has turned away from Him and found benefit? Or met with one of His aims?

Have you heard the words of the poet:

I came to you as a visitor at night, and every time I approached your door, I stumbled over my own weaknesses.

Chapter on the Necessity of Respecting Sharia Limits and Some Aspects of Ibn al-Jawzi's Life

---

Look, my son, at yourself regarding the boundaries. Notice how you guard them. Whoever guards them is preserved, and whoever neglects them is left. Let me remind you of some of my circumstances so that you may consider my efforts and ask for divine guidance for me.

Most of the blessings upon me were not due to my own merit, but rather from the providence of the Most Kind. I recall that I have had a lofty ambition since I was in the office, nearly for about six years, and I was among the elder boys. I was blessed with a fertile mind at a young age, surpassing the intellect of the elderly. I do not recall playing on a path with a child, nor laughing heartily. Even when I was around seven years old, I attended the gatherings of scholars, not opting for idle talk but seeking out scholars of hadith who spoke with long chains of narration. I memorized everything I heard and wrote it down when I returned home.

Blessed by Our Mentor Abu al-Fadl ibn Nasr, May Allah Have Mercy on Him

He used to carry me to the scholars, and he would make me listen to "al-Musnad" and other major books. I did not know what was expected of me, and he corrected me until I reached maturity. He handed down his steadfastness to me, and I remained with him until Allah took his soul. Through him, I attained knowledge of Hadith and transmission.

Childhood Days by the Tigris

While other children used to descend to the Tigris and watch the bridge, during my childhood, I took a book and sat beside the bank, engrossed in knowledge.

Inspired by Asceticism

Then I was inspired by asceticism. I observed fasting, focused on minimizing worldly pursuits, and disciplined myself to endure patience. I persisted, dedicated myself, and embraced wakefulness. I loved vigilance and did not content myself with just one aspect of knowledge. I listened to jurisprudence, sermons, and hadiths, following the examples of ascetics. Then I studied language and did not neglect anyone who secludes themselves or preaches, nor any stranger who attended.

Upholding Truth in Every Matter

Whenever two matters were presented to me, I upheld what is right. Allah perfected my plans and rewarded me with what was best for me. He repelled my enemies, jealous people, and those who plotted against me. He provided me with means of knowledge and granted me earnings unexpectedly. He endowed me with understanding, quick memory, and quality composition. I lacked nothing from the world but was granted sufficiency and more. He placed acceptance of my words in the hearts of people above the limit, and my words settled in their minds without doubt. I guided about two hundred People of the Book to Islam under my guidance, and more than a hundred thousand repented in my gatherings. I have refuted over twenty thousand misconceptions that the ignorant perpetuate.

Seeking Knowledge from Scholars

I used to seek out scholars to hear Hadith, fearing that my breath might cease before my enemies overtook me. I would spend mornings without food and evenings without anything, but Allah did not humiliate me before anyone. Instead, He facilitated my sustenance for the preservation of my dignity. If I were to elaborate on my circumstances, the explanation would be lengthy. Now you see what my situation has come to, summed up in one statement from Allah: "And fear Allah, and Allah teaches you." [Quran 2:282]

Urgency in Repentance, Regret, and Making Up for Lost Time

Pay attention, my son, to yourself and regret the negligence of your past. Strive to catch up with the righteous as long as time permits and nourish your branch while it is still moist. Remember the hours that have slipped away; they suffice as a lesson where the pleasure of laziness vanished, and opportunities for virtues were missed. The righteous predecessors used to cherish every virtue and weep over missing even one of them.

Examples of Regret and Reflection

Ibrahim ibn Adham, may Allah have mercy on him, once visited a sick worshipper who was crying while looking at his feet. When asked why he was crying, he replied, "These two feet did not get dusty in the path of Allah." Another person was asked why he was crying, and he said, "I regret a day I spent in silence and a night I let slip away."

Value of Time and Every Breath

Understand, my son, that days unfold into hours, hours into breaths, and each breath is a treasure. Beware of wasting a breath on something trivial, lest you see on the Day of Judgment an empty treasure chest and regret. A man once said to Aamir ibn Abd Qais, "Wait, I want to speak to you!" Aamir replied, "Hold back the sun."

Seizing Moments of Opportunity

People once gathered around Ma'ruf al-Karkhi, may Allah have mercy on him, and he said to them, "Do you wish to rise? For the angel who controls the sun never rests." The Hadith states, "Whoever says

'SubhanAllah wa bihamdihi' (Glory be to Allah and Praise Him), a palm tree is planted for him in Paradise." Consider how much the waster of hours misses out on palm trees.

Examples of Diligence from the Salaf

The Salaf used to seize moments diligently. Kahmas ibn al-Hasan al-Tamimi used to complete the Quran three times daily and nightly. Forty men from the Salaf used to perform Fajr prayer with the ablution of Isha. Rabia al-Adawiyya used to stay awake all night, and when dawn approached, she would sigh lightly and say to herself, "Sleeping in the graves is long."

Chapter on the Shortness of Worldly Life and the Necessity of Seizing It

Whoever contemplates the world before entering it perceives a long duration. But upon reflection after entering it, perceives it to be short. Know that dwelling in the graves is lengthy. Reflecting on the Day of Judgment, one realizes it spans fifty thousand years. Reflecting on eternity in Paradise or Hell, one understands it has no end. Returning to contemplate the remaining time in the world, let's say sixty years, thirty of which are spent sleeping and around fifteen in childhood. If you calculate what remains, most of it is consumed in desires, indulgences, and worldly gains. When one strives for the Hereafter, they often find hypocrisy and heedlessness therein. So, what are you buying with eternal life, when the price is these fleeting hours?

Chapter on Dispelling Despair and Embracing Diligence and Action

D o not despair of the good you missed due to negligence. Many have awakened after long periods of neglect and slumber. Sheikh Abu Hakim narrated to me about Qadi al-Qudat Abu al-Hasan Ali ibn Muhammad al-Damghani, may Allah have mercy on him, saying: "In my youth, I wasted time in idleness, neglecting knowledge. Abu Abdullah Muhammad ibn Ali al-Damghani then advised me, 'I will not stay with you forever. Take twenty dinars, open a bakery, and earn!' I replied, 'What is this talk?' He said, 'Open a dairy shop!' I said, 'Are you saying this to me, the son of the Chief Qadi Abu Abdullah al-Damghani?' He asked, 'Do you truly love knowledge?' I replied, 'Remind me of the lesson in an hour.' He reminded me, and I turned to diligently pursue knowledge, and Allah granted me success."

Anecdotes of Transformation Through Vigilance

Some companions of Abu Muhammad Abd al-Rahman ibn Muhammad al-Halwani, may Allah have mercy on him, told me: "My father passed away when I was twenty-one years old, known for idleness. I went to collect dues from residents of a house I had inherited. I heard them saying, 'The organizer has come.' They referred to me this way! I went to my mother and said, 'If you seek me, find me at the mosque of Sheikh Abu al-Khattab.' I remained committed, and soon became a judge."

Advice on Vigilance at Dawn and Avoidance of Worldly Matters

Restrict yourself, my son, to vigilance at dawn and avoid discussing worldly matters. The righteous predecessors, may Allah have mercy on them, did not engage in worldly affairs at that time. When you awaken from sleep, say: "All praise is due to Allah who has given us life after He caused us to die, and to Him is the resurrection. All praise is due to Allah who holds the heavens from falling upon the earth except by His permission. Indeed, Allah is Kind and Merciful to people."

Ritual Purity and the Dawn Prayer

Then perform ablution, observe the Sunnah of Fajr prayer, and leave for the mosque with humility. On your way, say: "O Allah, I ask You by the right of those who ask of You and by my walking towards You. I have not come out with evil intentions, vanity, or seeking fame. I have come out to avoid Your displeasure and seek Your pleasure. I ask You to protect me from the Fire and forgive my sins, for none forgives sins except You."

Observing Prayer on the Right Side of the Imam

After completing the prayer, say: "La ilaha illallah wahdahu la sharika lahu, lahul mulk wa lahul hamd wa huwa 'ala kulli shay'in qadir" ten times.

Then, say tasbih ten times, tahmid ten times, and takbir ten times.

Recite Ayat al-Kursi and supplicate to Allah for the acceptance of your prayer. If feasible, remain seated in remembrance of Allah until sunrise and its elevation.

Chapter on Daily Rituals

Engage in various fields of knowledge, focusing primarily on correcting Quranic recitation and studying jurisprudence. If you finish your lessons by mid-morning, perform eight rak'ahs of Duha prayer. Afterwards, occupy yourself with reading or transcription until Asr prayer.

Return to your studies after Asr until Maghrib prayer. Pray two rak'ahs after Maghrib, reciting portions of the Quran therein. After Isha prayer, return to your studies.

Prostration at Night

Lie down and say tasbih thirty-three times, tahmid thirty-three times, and takbir thirty-four times. Say: "Allahumma qini 'adhabaka yawma tajma'u 'ibadak."

Upon Awakening

Upon opening your eyes, perform ablution, and pray as much as possible in the darkness of the night. Ideally, start with two light rak'ahs, followed by two rak'ahs with longer Quranic recitations. Return to your studies, as knowledge is superior to all optional acts.

Chapter on Seclusion and Knowledge

Embrace seclusion, for it is the foundation of all goodness. Beware of the company of the wicked; let your companions be books and contemplation of the biographies of the pious predecessors. Do not delve into new knowledge until you have mastered what came before it. Glance at the lives of those who excelled in knowledge and action, and do not settle for less.

Know that knowledge elevates even the most humble. Many scholars were of unknown lineage and unremarkable appearance. Ata' ibn Abi Rabah was dark-skinned and unattractive. During his caliphate, Sulayman ibn Abd al-Malik brought his sons to learn about rituals from Ata', who was indifferent towards them. Upon this, Caliph Sulayman said to his sons, "Stand up and do not slacken or be lazy in seeking knowledge, for I have never felt more humbled before anyone than in the presence of him."

The Virtue of Piety

Strive, my son, to protect your honor from exposure to worldly pursuits and the humiliation they bring. Contentment is a source of strength, for it is said: "Whoever is content with bread and onions will not be enslaved by anyone."

An Arab once visited Basra and asked, "Who is the master of this city?" He was told, "Al-Hasan al-Basri." He asked further, "By what has he become their leader?" They replied, "He renounced his worldly possessions, and they became dependent on his knowledge."

Know, my son, that your grandfather was wealthy, leaving behind thousands of dinars. Your father, however, was a child, and that wealth was spent on him until he reached maturity. After that, he lived in one house and rented out another. Later, he was given about twenty dinars, which were said to be his entire inheritance. I took those dinars, bought books with them, sold the two houses, and spent the proceeds on seeking knowledge. Nothing was left of the money, and your grandfather did not humiliate himself in pursuit of the world like others. He did not travel through lands seeking favors from the affluent; his affairs were conducted with dignity. "And whoever fears Allah - He will make for him a way out and provide for him from where he does not expect." [Quran 65:2-3]

The Superiority of Piety

My son, when true piety is established, you will see all goodness. The pious do not seek the admiration of people or expose themselves to actions that harm their faith. "And whoever safeguards the limits set by Allah - it is those who are the truly guarded."

The Prophet (peace be upon him) said to Ibn Abbas (may Allah be pleased with them both), "Safeguard Allah's commands, and He will safeguard you. Safeguard Allah's commands, and you will find Him in front of you."

Know, my son, that when Yunus (peace be upon him) had nothing but piety as his provision, it saved him from distress. Allah says, "And had he not been of those who exalt Allah, he would have remained inside its belly until the Day they are resurrected." [Quran 37:143-144]

In contrast, when Pharaoh lacked any good provision, he found no sincere support in his distress. It was said to him, "Now? And you had disobeyed [Him] before?" [Quran 10:91]

Thus, establish treasures of goodness through piety whose effects you will feel. It is narrated, "There is no youth who fears Allah in his youth except that Allah elevates him in his later years."

Allah says, "And when he reached his maturity and became firmly established, We gave him wisdom and knowledge. And thus do We reward the doers of good." [Quran 12:22]

Know, my son, that among the most faithful treasures are averting the gaze from what is unlawful, restraining the tongue from idle talk, observing boundaries, and preferring Allah's pleasure over personal desires. Remember the story of the three individuals trapped in a cave, whose supplications were answered due to their righteousness.

Sufyan al-Thawri (may Allah have mercy on him) once saw a vision in which he was asked, "What has Allah done with you?" He replied, "I found myself placed in the grave, then suddenly I was before the Lord of the worlds. I was commanded to enter Paradise, and I entered. Then I heard someone saying, 'Sufyan, do you remember the day you preferred Allah over your desires?' I said, 'Yes.' Then the trays of gifts from Paradise were brought to me."

Chapter on the Harmony between Knowledge and Action

Strive, my son, to elevate your aspirations towards perfection. Some individuals were renowned for their asceticism, while others were occupied with knowledge. Rare are those who combined complete knowledge with exemplary action. Know that I have studied the Tabi'een and those who followed them, and I found no one more complete in four individuals: Sa'id ibn al-Musayyib, Sufyan al-Thawri, Al-Hasan al-Basri, and Ahmad ibn Hanbal. They were men whose aspirations surpassed ours. The early generations had many such individuals with lofty ambitions. If you wish to learn about their lives, read "Sifat al-Safwa" or delve into the biographies of Sa'id, Sufyan, and Ahmad ibn Hanbal. I have compiled books about each of them.

Chapter on the Virtue of Memorization and Truthfulness

Know, my son, that I have authored a hundred books. Among them are "Tafsir al-Kabir," spanning twenty volumes, "History," also twenty volumes, and "Tahdhib al-Musnad," another twenty volumes. The remaining books vary from large to small, totaling five volumes, two volumes, three volumes, and so on. These compilations should suffice you, eliminating the need to borrow books and gather efforts for writing. Focus on memorization, for it is the foundation, and practice is the profit. Be sincere in both seeking refuge with Allah and in your dealings, observing His limits. Allah says, "If you support Allah, He will support you" [Quran 47:7], "So remember Me; I will remember you" [Quran 2:152], "And fulfill My covenant, I will fulfill your covenant" [Quran 2:40].

Chapter on the Blessing and Benefit of Combining Knowledge with Action

Beware of stopping at the mere appearance of knowledge without acting upon it. Those who approached rulers and sought worldly gains neglected the application of their knowledge, thus depriving themselves of blessings and benefits.

Chapter on Good Intentions with Action

Avoid occupying yourself with worship devoid of knowledge. Many ascetics and mystics strayed from guidance because they acted without knowledge. Adorn yourself with two beautiful garments: one that does not make you conspicuous among worldly people with its elevation, and another that does not diminish your status among ascetics with its simplicity. Hold yourself accountable for every glance, word, and step, as you are responsible for them. The benefit others derive from your knowledge depends on how effectively you act upon it. If a preacher does not act upon his knowledge, his admonitions will slip away from hearts like water slips from a rock. Therefore, do not preach except with a sincere intention, do not walk except with a sincere intention, and do not eat except with a sincere intention. By studying the manners of the early righteous predecessors, the matter will become clear to you.

Chapter on Beneficial Books

You should read "Minhaj al-Muridin" for it guides your conduct, making it your constant companion and teacher. Consider "Said al-Khatir," as it provides practical insights that will rectify both your religious and worldly affairs. Memorize "Jannat al-Nazar" as it enriches your understanding of jurisprudence. If you turn to "Al-Hada'iq," you will gain access to the majority of Hadith literature. When you explore "Al-Kashf," it reveals to you what is concealed in Sahih al-Bukhari and Sahih Muslim. Avoid being preoccupied with exegesis books authored by non-Arabs, as "Al-Mughni" and "Zad al-Masir" render unnecessary any additional commentaries. As for the collections of sermons I have compiled for you, they suffice as a fundamental resource.

Chapter on Patience and Tolerance

Maintain good interaction with people while withdrawing from them when necessary. Solitude offers relief from the mingling of undesirable elements and preserves dignity. A preacher, especially, should not be seen in a disheveled state, walking in markets, or laughing, so that people may hold him in high regard and benefit from his teachings.

If you are compelled to interact with people, do so with patience towards them. If you uncover their shortcomings, you will not be able to bear being with them. Ensure you fulfill the rights of everyone entitled to them—whether spouse, child, or relative. Reflect on how each hour of your day is spent and bid farewell to it in the noblest manner possible. Do not neglect yourself; accustom it to the best and most virtuous deeds. Send to the grave what will please you on the day of reckoning. As it has been said:

"O you who were preoccupied with your worldly life, And were deceived by long hope, Death comes suddenly, And the grave is the container of deeds."

Chapter on Upholding Rights and Considering Consequences

Give each person their due rights, whether spouse, child, or relative. Monitor how each hour of your time is spent, ensuring it is used wisely. Do not neglect yourself; accustom it to the best and most virtuous deeds. Plan your affairs carefully, as Allah is the Best of Planners. Spend your wealth wisely without extravagance, so you will not need to depend on others. Preserving wealth prevents indebtedness, and leaving behind a good inheritance for your heirs is better than needing others.

Chapter on the Honor of Lineage

My son, know that we are descendants of Abu Bakr al-Siddiq (may Allah be pleased with him), and our father is al-Qasim ibn Muhammad ibn Abu Bakr (may Allah be pleased with him). Their biographies are documented in the book "Sifat al-Safwa." Our predecessors were engaged in trade and commerce, and none was granted the ambition to seek knowledge more than me. Now, this responsibility has fallen upon you. Strive not to disappoint my hopes in what I have wished for you.

I entrust you to Allah, and from Him I seek guidance for you in knowledge and action. This is the extent of my effort in advising you, and there is no power or strength except with Allah, the Most High, the Most Great.

All praise is due to Allah, the Lord of the worlds, and peace and blessings be upon our Prophet Muhammad, his family, and his companions.